# Medieval Scandinavian Armies (1)

## 1100–1300

D Lindholm & D Nicolle · Illustrated by Angus McBride

*Series editor* Martin Windrow

First published in Great Britain in 2003 by Osprey Publishing,
Midland House, West Way, Botley, Oxford OX2 0PH, UK
44-02 23rd St, Suite 219, Long Island City, NY 11101, USA
Email: info@ospreypublishing.com

Transferred to digital print on demand 2010

First published 2003
3rd impression 2008

Printed and bound by Cadmus Communications, USA

A CIP catalogue record for this book is available from the British Library

ISBN: 978 1 84176 505 1

Series Editor: Martin Windrow
Design by Alan Hamp
Index by Alan Rutter
Maps by David Nicolle
Originated by Electronic Page Company, Cwmbran, UK

**Artist's note**

Readers may care to note that the original paintings from which the colour plates in this book were prepared are available for
private sale. All reproduction copyright whatsoever is retained by the Publisher. Enquiries should be addressed to:

Scorpio Gallery
PO Box 475
Hailsham
East Sussex
BN27 2SL
UK

The Publishers regret that they can enter into no correspondence upon this matter.

**The Woodland Trust**

Osprey Publishing is supporting the Woodland Trust, the UK's leading woodland conservation charity, by funding the
dedication of trees.

**www.ospreypublishing.com**

# MEDIEVAL SCANDINAVIAN ARMIES (1) AD 1100–1300

## INTRODUCTION

THE MILITARY HISTORY of medieval Scandinavia can be divided into several parts. The first is sometimes known as the pre-Viking period of the so-called Dark Age, which ended when Scandinavian sea-raiders suddenly descended upon several of their neighbours in the closing years of the 8th century AD. The widely studied period which followed is generally known as the Viking Age. It ended in the late 11th century, by which time Christianity had arrived in much, though by no means all of the Scandinavian world.

The medieval periods which followed the Late Viking Age have attracted much less attention amongst military historians outside Scandinavia. In some respects the 12th to 14th centuries formed another distinct period. Yet this was a time of considerable and important change within Scandinavia, which is why it has been divided into two sub-sections for the purposes of our two books on Medieval Scandinavian Armies. The second book will focus on the military character of Scandinavia in the 15th and early 16th centuries. This was the time of the Union of Kalmar when Norway, Sweden and Denmark shared a single monarch (1395–1523), and which witnessed the Union Wars.

\* \* \*

During the 12th century most Scandinavian armies were based upon the concept of the *ledung* or 'ship's levy', which was a relic of the Viking Age, and upon the assembling of larger armies under a king or other war chief. This system remained in use in Sweden until the end of the 12th century. In Denmark, however, the adoption of a Western European feudal levy and the concept of feudal service appeared more quickly. It was also accepted more thoroughly than elsewhere in Scandinavia as a result of Denmark's close contacts with neighbouring Germany.

The 13th century saw further development of the feudal system, a process that would continue throughout the 14th century. However, in Scandinavia the so-called feudal system took on a distinct and almost unique character which set it apart from most other Western European models. For example, the greater part of the Swedish army continued to consist of a levy of peasants and free men who mustered with their own weapons.

Part of a tapestry from Skog church, Sweden. Though made in the Christian 12th century it still portrays three pagan Norse gods: from left to right, Odin, Thor and Freyr. (National Historical Museum, Stockholm)

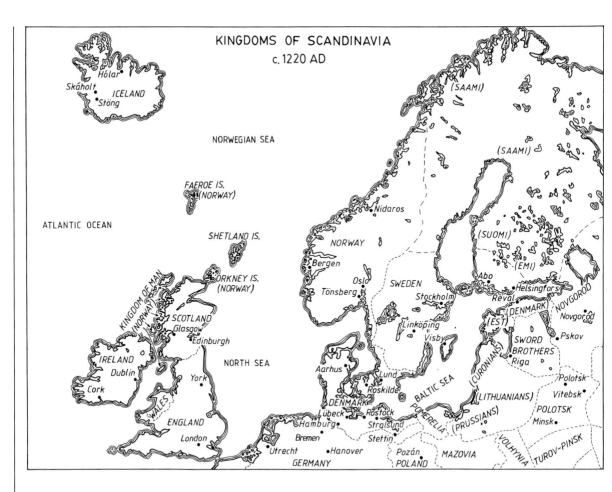

Furthermore, these men would only fight under specific, previously agreed circumstances, which usually involved defending a clearly defined territory – normally close to where such men had their own homes.

During this period the aristocracy played a minor role as far as the real fighting forces of Scandinavia were concerned. Another interesting feature that certainly set Scandinavian armies apart from those seen in most other parts of Western Europe was the continuing close links between different social classes during the stresses of warfare, and the mutual respect which they showed to one another; the arrogance of the supposedly typical feudal knight was totally absent. Generally speaking, these medieval Scandinavian armies were small compared to those seen in continental Europe. They almost never numbered more than 4,000 fighting men, and were usually around 500 strong.

In terms of military equipment, there was remarkably little change from the mid-11th to late 13th centuries, probably because of the under-developed economies of these countries as well as their distinctive social characteristics. One new weapon did arrive, however, and would have a lasting impact: this was the crossbow, which became firmly identified with Scandinavian peasant militias, to such an extent that by the end of the medieval period every free man owned a crossbow.

Once again, the position in Denmark was slightly different from that elsewhere in medieval Scandinavia. This was, of course, a result of Denmark's close political and economic links with the German Empire.

Such links continued to influence developments in Denmark throughout the medieval period. As a result new military ideas, including those concerning tactics and weaponry, appeared in Denmark at an earlier date than in Sweden, Norway and distant Iceland. During this period Finland was, for all practical purposes, part of Sweden; the only exceptions were those southern and south-eastern regions of Finland whose control was disputed between Sweden and the Russian Principality of Novgorod. The northern parts of what is now Finland were an 'outback' region inhabited by tribesmen having little contact with the civilised states of Scandinavia or Russia.

Prior to the 14th century Norway had closer links with Sweden than with Denmark. Nevertheless, Norway played only a minor role in medieval warfare, while the major players remained Denmark and Sweden. On the other hand it is important to note that the German-based Hanseatic League of merchant cities would play an increasingly important military and naval role, both economically and as suppliers of men and money. This League was officially established in the 13th century and did not reach full development until the 14th century. Nevertheless, German merchants were already settling on the Swedish island of Gotland where they founded the fortified trading city of Visby in the second half of the 12th century. German merchants subsequently settled in various Norwegian ports during the 13th century, followed by lodgements in other parts of Sweden where they played an important part in the rise of Stockholm and Kalmar.

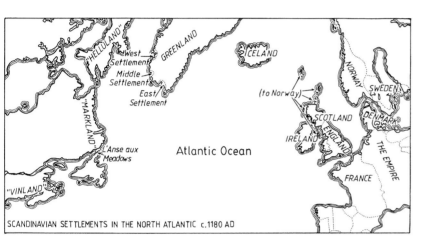

SCANDINAVIAN SETTLEMENTS IN THE NORTH ATLANTIC c.1180 AD

# CHRONOLOGY

| | |
|---|---|
| **1030** | Olaf Haraldsson is killed at the battle of Stiklestad, to be recognised later as a Christian saint. |
| **c.1035** | Earl Thorfinn of Orkney seizes control of northern Scotland. |
| **1042** | End of Danish rule in England. |
| **1043** | King Magnus the Good defeats pagan Slav Wends. |
| **1047–64** | Conflict between Harald Hardrada of Norway and Svein Estrithson of Denmark. |
| **1066** | Harald Hardrada is killed at the battle of Stamford Bridge in England. |
| **1069** | Svein Estrithson of Denmark invades England. |
| **1075** | Last Danish invasion of England. |
| **1075** | Godred Crovan unites the Norse Kingdoms of Man and the Hebrides. |

| | |
|---|---|
| 1086 | Death of King Knut of Denmark, to be cannonised as a saint in 1101. |
| 1095 | Scottish king recognises Norwegian sovereignty over the Hebrides. |
| 1100 | Period of raids by Slav Obodrites on Danish territory. |
| 1103 | King Magnus Bareleg of Norway killed while raiding Ireland. |
| 1107–11 | King Sigurd of Norway goes on Crusade to Palestine. |
| 1123 | King Sigurd Magnússon of Norway plunders the Kalmar region of Sweden. |
| 1126 | Norse communities in Greenland receive their first bishop. |
| 1129 | Lord Knut, son of Danish King Eric 'Ever Good', invited to become the first king of the Slav Obodrites under German suzereinty. |
| 1130 | Death of King Sigurd Magnússon of Norway. |
| 1130–84 | Intermittent civil wars in Norway. |
| 1131–57 | Intermittent civil war in Denmark; Wendish and other Slav pirates take opportunity to raid Danish lands. |
| 1147 | Danish Crusades attack pagan Wends on southern shore of Baltic Sea. |
| 1153 | King Harald Eystein of Norway raids the east coast of England. |
| 1155–70 | Civil wars in many parts of Scandinavia. |
| 1156 | Somerled, a local chief of mixed Norse and Scots origin, seizes the southern Hebrides from King Godred II of the Kingdom of Man. |
| 1157 | Valdemar I becomes king of Denmark; start of the 'Valdemar Age'. |
| 1160 | Approximate date of the death of King Erik of Sweden, later regarded as a national saint. |
| 1169 | Danes occupy Rügen islands and begin their expansion in the Baltic. |
| 1177 | Sverrir Sigurdsson from the Faroe Islands arrives in Norway to lead a largely peasant army in revolt; becomes sole king of Norway in **1184** and establishes an Anglo-Norman style of centralised government. |
| 1180–82 | Unsuccessful revolt against the Danish king and the church authorities in Skåne. |
| 1191–97 | Danish Crusaders invade Finland and Estonia. |
| 1201 | Swedish invasion of Novgorod in north-western Russia. |
| 1202 | Bishop Jón Smyrill of Greenland visits Rome. |
| 1206 | Danish Crusade against the Estonian Ösel island. |
| 1210 | Danish Crusaders attack Prussians. |
| 1219–20 | Danish Crusaders invade northern Estonia and build Tallinn castle. |
| 1220 | Swedish Crusade against Estonian coast. |
| 1227 | Denmark defeated at the battle of Bornhöved; collapse of the Danish Baltic empire. |
| 1238 | Part of the territory of the abolished Crusader Order of Sword Brethren in Estonia handed over to Denmark. |
| 1240 | First Swedish Crusade to Finland; Swedish and Finn force defeated by Novgorod at the battle of the River Neva. |
| 1242 | Defeat of a Crusader army, including a Danish contingent from Estonia, by the Russian Prince Alexander Nevskii at the battle of Lake Peipus. |
| 1243 | Estonian uprising against Danish rule. |
| 1251 | Birger, regent for his son King Valdemar of Sweden, hires |

**Simple incised stone effigial slab of a supposed 'Crusader' knight from Vejerslev, Denmark, 12th century. Note the cross on his helmet.**

foreign mercenaries to crush the Folkungs or Swedish aristocratic party.

**1261** Greenland becomes an 'overseas territory' of Norway; end of the autonomous republican government of the Greenland settlements.

**1263** Iceland becomes an 'overseas territory' of Norway; end of the autonomous republican government of Iceland; Scots defeat King Hakon IV of Norway at the battle of Largs.

**1266** Norway cedes the Hebrides and Isle of Man to Scotland.

**1274** Magnus Ladulås leads a revolt against King Valdemar of Sweden and is acknowledged as king.

**1277** Naval expedition to explore the western coast of Greenland sets out from Gardar.

**1293** Third Finnish Crusade by Sweden extends Swedish control to the shore of Lake Ladoga, leading to conflict with the Russian Principality of Novgorod (frontier finally agreed in 1323).

# SOCIAL & MILITARY ORGANISATION

The differences between medieval Scandinavian society and that of the rest of Europe can easily be overstated. Such variations largely reflected the survival of older forms of social organisation in Scandinavia for longer than they did in most other parts of Western Europe. There were also notable variations within Scandinavia between the three kingdoms of Denmark, Norway and Sweden, as well as between the more developed south and the still essentially tribal far north.

While Western Europe was gradually transformed along feudal lines, Scandinavia retained older forms of kinship-based society. Only much later was anything approaching the concept of a divinely approved kingship accepted, along with a landed aristocracy that held its lands from the king in return for service. In late 11th and 12th century Scandinavia, and even later in some regions, close family bonds and extended kinship groups remained the glue that bound social units together.

There were no lords or kings who held legal dominion over a family or group of families. Instead there existed voluntary ties whereby a social group or an individual offered allegiance or service in exchange for 'gifts'. In fact 'gift giving' remained a central feature in pre-feudal society. The original gift-giving society had its roots in the Bronze

The ruins of the medieval church at Hvalsey near Qaqortoq in Greenland. This was one of the most important locations in what was known as the Eastern Settlement during the medieval period. (Greenland Tourist Office photograph)

7

Two carved wooden panels from the 12th century timber church at Hylestad in Norway. They are believed to illustrate the stories of an ancient Nordic hero. (Universitetets Oldsaks Samling, Oslo)

Age and had probably been the dominant form of social organisation throughout most of Europe. Once the idea that kingship came from God was added to this ancient concept, it eventually led to a social model in which the king owned all land but then gave it away in exchange for service – namely feudalism.

In early medieval Scandinavia the gift-giving was generally made possible by raiding neighbours who were outside the circle of gift-givers and receivers, or by the taking of tribute from weaker neighbours. Successful raiding virtually came to an end during the Late Viking Age of the 11th century, because the former victims were now strong enough to make raiding unprofitable. Consequently it became necessary for would-be Scandinavian rulers to look elsewhere to fund gifts to their followers.

This had two effects. The first was that the number of men in locally recruited Scandinavian armies decreased, since it was no longer possible to attract them with the promise of plunder. The second was that the king had to rely on his own personal domain as his primary source of cash income. This severely limited his possibilities when it came to such activities as major building projects. Consequently the rulers welcomed the Church's doctrine that kings ruled with a divine mandate, and were thus overlords of all economic assets as well as all their subjects.

The friction between nobility and king that existed throughout medieval Western Europe, including Scandinavia, largely stemmed from the fact that the king could now claim ownership over all the land. In response the aristocracy often maintained, quite truthfully, that their families had held such land for generations, often from times before kings came on the scene. The result was that kings became dependent upon the goodwill of the aristocracy and on being accepted by them, since in practice the only land that the ruler could give as a gift or in return for services was the land of his own personal domain. Unfortunately that land was also vital as a source of royal cash revenue. In fact, Scandinavian monarchs generally remained chronically short of money well into the post-medieval or Renaissance period, even more so than most other European kings.

**Land, wealth and power**
Within Scandinavian society there existed distinct socio-economic groups. First came the free landholders, who ranged from those farming small areas to those owning large tracts. In the latter case the families in question formed the oldest nobility in Scandinavia, their status being based upon acres owned rather than on abstract legal or social criteria. If was from this class that the earliest kings emerged, usually being members of the most prominent groups who gained lordship through being elected by their peers. Their landholders would then

automatically be bound to the new king through their loyalty to him as their direct overlord.

Here it is important to note that no legal structure yet existed to define and govern such allegiances. Allegiance operated on a simple kinship basis, and also through the gift-giving of superiors to inferiors outside the superior's immediate kinship group. What made Scandinavia distinctive was the fact that such a system survived in a largely undiluted version for considerably longer than elsewhere in Europe.

Below the great landowners and those of their kinsmen who worked their land would be a class known as the *Landbor*. These men did not own the land they farmed but rented it from the owner. Such families would be linked by bonds of loyalty and economic necessity to the landowner for as long as they tilled his land. On the other hand, it is important to notice that this distinctive Scandinavian class were not serfs, but remained free men. Some were wealthy enough to clear new land from the forest or wasteland and thus to become significant landowners in their own right. These men would also go to war in support of their overlord.

**Fortified tower known as the** ***Kastel,*** **next to the church at Gammelgarn on the island of Gotland. It was built in the 12th century to serve as a local refuge.**

Below the Landbor came a class of serfs. In Scandinavia the status of serfdom was legally abolished in the 14th century, though its limiting realities survived much longer. For practical purposes the poorest of the Landbor class remained effectively serfs because of the high rents that they had to pay. Furthermore they were unable to move to another district because of the taxes that had to be paid, especially as they found it very difficult to generate any other form of income.

## The political and military role of the Church

Denmark was the first Scandinavian country to become Christian, followed by Norway, Iceland, and lastly Sweden and Finland. With Christianity came priests, monks, literacy, scholarship, and the concept of divinely ordained kingship with the Church as the dispenser of royal legitimacy. The Church also created its own power base. This became a marriage of convenience between the newly established kings and the Church, with the latter supplying the ideology that kingship was handed down from God to a divinely appointed ruler, who must therefore be obeyed. This paradoxically made the monarch dependent upon the goodwill of the Church's local representatives – namely the bishops and archbishops who provided legitimacy to kingship.

Christianity was actually brought to Scandinavia from three different directions. Traces of Orthodox Christianity from the East have been found along the Baltic coast. Meanwhile Norway was heavily influenced by English and Irish missionaries, while Denmark and southern Sweden were Christianised from northern Germany. This process helped to establish many of the trade links and family ties that developed during the Middle Ages. At the same time Norway focused its attentions in the direction of Iceland and Greenland; Sweden looked towards the Baltic, and Denmark looked south towards Germany.

In the Early and High Middle Ages of Scandinavia, bishops came from the leading families, and many were not what modern observers

**Carved panels on a wooden chair from Blaked Farm in Low Oppland, c.1200. (University Museum, Oslo)**

would regard as typical 'men of the cloth'. On several occasions Scandinavian bishops ritually placed their robes and mitre upon the altar of their cathedral and then put on their armour to fight at the head of an army (the last time this happened was in 15th century Sweden). This helps to explain why bishops built such a significant proportion of Scandinavia's castles. They also maintained armed retinues rivalling those of the kings themselves, both in size and the quality of their military equipment.

This warlike tendency went so far that the right of bishops to maintain armoured knights as their own retainers was ended in Sweden during the 13th century. During the strife that regularly erupted between the aristocracy and the crown, the Church never stood entirely on the sidelines. These occasions also demonstrated that ties of kinship played a major part in a churchman's decision to support one side or the other. As a result, different Swedish bishops often supported different sides.

The support of the Church was keenly sought during these confrontations, being paid for in land and donations. Meanwhile powerful aristocratic leaders did what they could to ensure that a suitable younger brother obtained an influential position within the Church hierarchy. In Denmark the situation seems to have been more stable, perhaps as a result of a succession of strong kings who asserted the power and the rights of the crown from the start. Yet this did not prevent Danish bishops from playing a central role in various struggles for power.

Below the bishops and higher clergy were the priests and monks. The Cistercian Order was perhaps the greatest force for innovation in medieval Scandinavia. It introduced many of the skills that proved useful in the construction of fortifications, while on a more peaceful level the Order's monks cared for the sick, as well as introducing new plants, reading and writing.

\* \* \*

The Viking Age system of conflict resolution centred on the *Tinget,* which was a gathering of all free men. Here disputes were arbitrated by a number of selected *Lagmän.* These men were well versed in the traditions of how certain issues should be resolved; in fact, the system was almost based upon the concept of legal precedent. A Lagmän would, of course, gain considerable influence, and they provided an aristocracy alongside the greatest landowners.

It is interesting to note that in medieval Scandinavia conflicts between the nobility and the king probably arose from the Viking Age concept of the equality of all free men. Kings, nobles and Lagmän were initially regarded as being the 'first amongst equals', and there was no sense of them being 'better' than a poor but free landowner. The strife engendered as a result of this concept then led to the establishment of a feudal aristocracy, which tried to limit the development of excessive royal power. Such conflicts continued right up to the 16th century when the first of what history knows as the Absolute Kings emerged. Paradoxically, the Scandinavian kingdoms then entered the 17th century with the most organised and powerful monarchies yet seen in Western Europe.

\*    \*    \*

There was considerable variation in the organisation of Scandinavian armies in the 11th and 12th centuries. These ranged from the war parties of hunter-gatherer communities in the far north, to the proto-feudal levy – which already existed in a very simple form in Denmark at the close of the Viking Age. Generally speaking, during the 11th, 12th and in some places even the 13th century, Scandinavian kings had to be acknowledged or accepted by an assembly of leading men or nobles. This was not necessarily the 'elective' system claimed by earlier historians; nevertheless, it is clear that rulers were still expected to seek the endorsement of the country's warrior aristocracy. In Sweden this would remain a continuing source of strife up to the 16th century. Such assemblies could also be held in several places. For example, the kings of Sweden summoned what was known as an *Eriksgata,* at which they would hope to be accepted by the nobles of each territory, such acceptance being indicated by acclaim – the shouting of approval.

During the 12th century there was considerable strife within Denmark and Norway. This took place as different political factions competed for power within established kingdoms which were not under threat of collapse. In Sweden the situation was different: there the kings were elected at a *Mora stenar* in accordance with a system that continued into the 14th century. Next the continental European concept of 'divinely ordained kingship' was established, and resulted in the holding of normal coronation ceremonies, firstly in 12th century Denmark, then in Norway, and finally in Sweden during the 13th century.

By the end of the 11th century Scandinavian kings could no longer rely on foreign adventures to assemble royal wealth or to attract fighters in their support. Such military enterprises could still be rewarding, but they were becoming more risky because other Baltic peoples were developing more effective forms of defence. In fact some non-Scandinavian Baltic peoples now began conducting their own raids, the Slavic Wends of what are now the coastal regions of north-eastern Germany and north-western Poland being particularly active.

Instead of raids for plunder, royal estates became the main source of royal revenue. Such revenues were relatively predictable but were also clearly limited, and generally placed an upper limit on the number of troops the king could field, since the monarch had to pay them himself. Expeditions abroad or outside the kingdom were conducted by the king and his own men, plus additional troops levied from tributary rulers or members of the nobility. If, on the other hand, the king's own territory was attacked, then all able

'The Massacre of the Innocents', illustrated on a gilded altar-front from Broddetorp in Västergötland. (National Historical Museum, Stockholm)

bodied men were legally expected to arm themselves and defend the kingdom. Needless to say, these men were also expected to be able to use their weapons effectively and to have had a certain amount of training. Other forms of support from the countryside could be in the form of providing or transporting supplies, or constructing fixed defences.

Another significant development was an increasing use of cavalry in Scandinavia from the second half of the 12th century. This was on a small scale, however, and many of these first cavalrymen were German mercenaries. One reason for this need to hire German cavalry may have been the character of the traditional Scandinavian horse breeds: though tough and well adapted to the harsh climate, these local horses were rather small. Furthermore their natural running gait made them excellent for peaceful riding, but very unsuitable as warhorses.

### Mercenaries, the *Lid* and the *Hird*

Another development during this period concerned the replacement of service in the feudal levy by a form of monetary payment, which a ruler could then use to hire professional mercenaries. Perhaps partly as a result, German military influences became increasingly more apparent, though not yet as strong as they would be during the 14th and 15th centuries. While the payment of taxes instead of feudal military service may have become normal by the late 12th century, however, the widespread introduction of such fees did not mean that the traditional levy of fighting men disappeared. What seems to have happened is that such proto-feudal levies were not needed as often as in earlier days when they had formed the only real means of defence.

Embroidered tapestry from Baldishols church, Norway. Although the knight looks very similar to those in 11th or 12th century sources from elsewhere in Western Europe, this Scandinavian tapestry actually dates from the 13th century. (Kunstindustrimuseet, Oslo)

This development was marked by a significant increase in royal authority, because the king became the only power in the realm with a professional standing army at his command. On the other hand, this should not be overstated; such forces tended to be small and still consisted largely of infantry, though led by knights. In Norway this levy remained the only effective standing force available to the king, probably because the terrain of Norway was singularly unsuited to mounted warfare. Consequently the presence of foreign mercenaries was less marked in Norway than elsewhere.

In Sweden and Denmark landholders who had their own military followers were exempted from taxes in return for bringing their men to fight for the king. Norway had a more selective system, in which exemption was only granted on the basis of agricultural land farmed by the nobleman in question. Land which was farmed by the nobleman's own subtenants continued to be taxed. The agents who collected such taxes remained a very important part of the royal government in both Sweden and Denmark throughout the Middle Ages, acting as the king's representatives in various parts of the kingdom.

The king in turn depended upon their acceptance and support right up to the 13th century. By then royal power had increased to such an extent that the ruler made direct agreements between himself and the nobility; such agreements set out the duties and privileges of the king and of the nobleman.

The Scandinavian aristocracy of the High and Later Middle Ages were descended from leading families that dominated the more densely populated areas during the closing decades of the Viking Age. In 11th century Norway land that had been given by the king as payment for services to him was already being inherited by such families. As was also the case in continental Western Europe, there was always a danger that powerful Scandinavian families might rebel and even attempt to seize power from the king. In an effort to prevent this happening, the noblemen were often made members of the Royal *Lid* or *Hird*. This Hird was a relic from the Viking Age; originally consisting of the armed followers of a king or chieftain, it was made up of his closest supporters and remained part of his personal household. Throughout the medieval period the Hird remained a functioning institution, providing regular personal contact between Hird members and their overlord and thus inhibiting rebellion.

## Councillors and administrators

Nevertheless, there were civil wars and low level strife in Scandinavia during the 12th century. Such conflicts were generally fought by military groups who were the only 'professional' forces in Scandinavia, their sizes varying considerably. In the Viking Age they could be as small as a single ship's crew, or as many as 20 or 30 crews totalling 300 to 400 fighting men. During the Middle Ages the word Hird was used to denote a family group or extended family that included non-blood relatives linked by marriage or in other ways. Meanwhile the word Lid came to have more strictly military connotations, while the Hird served not only as a military force but could also include priests or bishops. Some members of the Hird often remained in one place, performing administrative duties for the king, while others travelled with him around the country or on campaign. These partly or non-military members of the Hird became the nucleus of an emerging administrative class that reached full development at the end of the 13th century. During this process the Norwegian Hird adopted several hierarchical ranks originating from continental Europe. The *lendrmenn* or 'men given land by the king' became barons; below them were the knights or *riddare*, followed by the squires or *svenner*. Similar developments took place in Sweden and Denmark.

The Hird also provided the king with his royal council or *Riksråd*. Such councils gained considerable influence and importance during the second half of the 13th century, though there were differences between the Scandinavian

Carved wooden roundel from the church door at Valpjósstaóir in Iceland, made c.1200. The knight on the upper panel has a helmet with a nasal, cheek pieces and a neck protection. (National Museum, Reykjavik)

13

**Part of a fragmentary embroidered textile from Røn church, made c.1200. It appears to show dead warriors and part of a horse. (University Museum, Oslo)**

kingdoms. Whereas in Norway the Hird became an assembly of all noblemen, in Sweden and Denmark the aristocracies were much larger. As a result different sorts of assemblies emerged, where important matters such as war or major disputes could be settled. In Sweden this was called a *Herredag* and in Denmark a *Danhof.* Amongst the duties which fell to these councils was that of agreeing new taxation which the king claimed was needed to cover royal expenses for wars or large construction programmes. This division of authority would, however, provide fertile ground for strife during the 15th century.

In the Swedish countryside the king's representatives were called *Fogde.* They were responsible for collecting taxes, enforcing law and order, and ensuring that no rebellion was brewing. If the area in question included a fortified castle, the man who held this castle would often be entrusted with such provincial duties. A castle was an important military asset, so a trusted royal servant who was not a member of the nobility was normally put in charge of such fortifications.

In the cities of Scandinavia the system was different. If, for example, the city was connected to the Hanseatic League, it would be largely self-governing. Other less important cities, or those not associated with the Hanseatic League, normally had their own council, or were dominated by a resident nobleman whose personal domain included that town or city. The urban solutions used in Scandinavia varied considerably at different periods and places; generally speaking, however, the king's power was weaker in the cities than in the countryside. This was especially so in cities which had fortifications and which could, in effect, close their gates against the king.

\*　\*　\*

During the first half of the 13th century the system of military training for the Scandinavian nobility became the same as that seen elsewhere in continental Europe, just as the concept of knightly service as a mounted warrior also took hold. Higher demands were now made on the individual nobleman's military skills and consequently greater emphasis was placed on training with his horse and weapons. The system of sending young men to live in the households of relatives or influential friends where they would receive proper military training became widespread, especially in the higher strata of society. At the same time, however, it was not uncommon for such training to be carried out at home, under the supervision of a senior 'master at arms' or the most experienced of the *svennerna* (squires) in the castle. As far as members of the ordinary military levy were concerned, they were expected to learn the basics of how to use weapons as a part of growing up. Relatives or neighbours would teach young men at home in their spare time, to a standard adequate to defend a farm from robbers and fulfil the duties of levy service.

Two mounted warriors from the Lewis chess pieces, made in the Kingdom of the Isles during the 12th century. Like many of the foot soldiers in the set, both have helmets with pendant cheek and neck protections. (British Museum, London)

# WEAPONS & EQUIPMENT

### Northern Scandinavia 1100–1200

Between 1100 and 1200 considerable differences emerged between the equipment used in Sweden and Norway and that used in Denmark to the south. At the close of the 11th century almost all Scandinavian warriors still looked much like their Viking grandfathers, and nor was there much to set them apart from each other. The most important equipment remained the shield, spear and helmet. Some men had swords or axes, the latter being more common than the former. Some had mail armour, since good mail had become more available as a result of plundering expeditions. Although there is little evidence for indigenous production of mail within Scandinavia before the 15th century, local manufacture cannot be entirely discounted.

In Sweden and Norway the evidence indicates that the most common form of **helmet** in the 11th–12th centuries remained the conical type with a nose guard. Other types of helmet have also been found at Viking sites, and were clearly used by Scandinavian warriors; these included the distinctive Gjermundby-style helmet.

**Shields** used in the 11th century remained round and were usually of poplar or alder wood, their thickness varying between 1cm and 2.5cm (1 inch). Sometimes the best of these shields were constructed in glued layers with each layer placed at an angle to that beneath, the whole being covered with leather. However, this sturdy laminated form of construction was not common, and the thinner type of round shield was more widespread. The diameter of such shields varied from that of a hand-held buckler up to a maximum diameter of one metre (3.28 feet). The shield might be reinforced with an iron band around its rim, and from two to four iron bands across the face.

Later in the 12th century the kite-shaped shield came into use, but only by the minority of warriors who fought on horseback; the size of the fully developed kite shield normally made it too unwieldy for men on foot. As more effective body armour came into use, including rigid or semi-rigid plates, so later forms of the kite shield were adopted. These were shorter and usually had an almost or completely horizontal upper edge.

In Sweden and Norway the population were notably slower than in Denmark to take advantage of horses. As a result even men who owned horses generally preferred to ride to battle and then dismount to fight. This preference for infantry combat naturally became a drawback when facing the Danes. In Denmark mounted warriors were in fact introduced at a surprisingly early date, and by the beginning of the 12th century the concept of mounted combat was well established. A comparable process would not take place in Sweden until a hundred years later, and was even slower in Norway, as a natural consequence of local topographical conditions. For the same reasons a road system was also more developed in Denmark than in the northern regions.

The **body armour** used during this period differed according to location. By the early 11th century mail was in almost universal use, and this form of armour had, of course, been known during the Viking Age. On the other hand, early fragments found by archaeologists are so small that it is almost impossible to identify the shape of the garment from which they came. In such mail each ring or link engaged with four other

rings, resulting in a thick and sturdy mail shirt. Other patterns also existed, and sometimes the rings used in such mail could be very thin.

Scandinavian illustrations from the 11th and 12th centuries reveal that to some extent Sweden and Norway again lagged behind Denmark in the use of body armour. Furthermore, in these northern countries mail seems to have been restricted to the uppermost social classes, and even amongst the leading nobility it mostly consisted of mail shirts of varying lengths. For example, a knee-length *hauberk* appears on aristocratic seals such as that of Karl Döve in the last decade of the 12th century. In Denmark the adoption of more advanced forms of armour was much more rapid, and here the nobility clearly used the knee-length mail hauberk by the early 12th century. In this, Denmark was following the lead of neighbouring Germany.

In Scandinavia there is archaeological evidence that lamellar armour may have been in continuous use from the early Viking Age to the late Middle Ages. This would set Scandinavia apart from the rest of Western Europe. For example, fragments of lamellar armour are amongst other finds from 6th century sites in Valsgärde, which also include what appear to be arm or leg greaves made of iron splints. More recent archaeological finds at Birka in Mälaren point to the use of lamellar body armour in the 9th or 10th century. Amongst the abundant armour found in the grave pits at Visby, dating from 1361, there were no less than 25 coats-of-plates as well as several suits of lamellar armour of Eastern or non-European origin. It is highly likely that these lamellar armours were brought to Scandinavia as a result of trade and were kept in use for a long time.

**Swords** used during the Viking Age were not limited to the common Viking type with a standard pommel and straight, thick guard. This form of sword was used for cutting and was not a thrusting weapon; its blade lacked a sharp point and was balanced well forward, which gave power to a cut but was unsuitable for thrusting. Nor was the sword a weapon for the ordinary soldier, axes and spears being far more common.

Interestingly enough, it is in Finland that we find the earliest archaeological Scandinavian evidence for what later came to be known (inaccurately) as the 'Norman' sword. This had a more acute point and an almond-shaped pommel. It was also this design that later became the dominant form – though with several variations – up to the 13th century. Nevertheless, during this period it was not the blade that changed so much as the pommel and guard. New designs of sword which appeared in continental Europe soon found their way to Scandinavia. At the same time Scandinavia had its own domestic arms industry dating back at least to the Migration Period and Viking Age.

Another distinctive form of sword found in Norway and Sweden was a single-edged cutting weapon with a straight blade. It was very much like the later 'backsword' of England, and when furnished with a straight crossguard it was in many respects a large version of the *saex*. In this context it might be worth noting Scandinavia's close trading links with the Islamic world. The straight but single-edged *palash* or proto-sabre was the standard sword of the early medieval nomadic peoples of the steppes, while a heavier but still straight single-edged weapon was one of several forms in the early Islamic armies of the Middle East, Iran and Transoxania.

Detail from another 'Massacre of the Innocents', on a carved stone panel made at the end of the 13th century. One of Herod's soldiers (left centre) wears a scale cuirass, which has sometimes been seen as evidence that scale was used in Sweden at this time. (in situ, Cathedral, Linköping; Colette Nicolle photograph)

The **axe** was the weapon used by the majority of ordinary Scandinavian soldiers, because everybody had one readily available. In the earlier Viking Age the long-shafted war-axe almost became a distinguishing feature for Viking warriors. The same characteristic form of axe design persisted in Scandinavia during the subsequent High and Late Medieval centuries. Even as late as the 15th century, fully armoured knights were portrayed in battle wielding large two-handed axes. The axe was, of course, easy to use and cheap to manufacture, and most men would have had some experience of using one from working in forests or fields. The effectiveness of such medieval war-axes cannot be doubted, and modern experiments have shown that a two-handed axe will easily cleave a shield, a mail hauberk and even plate armour. Nevertheless, it remained an infantryman's weapon; it was not suitable for mounted warfare, even though several medieval illuminated manuscripts do show cavalrymen wielding axes with both hands. Normally the axe used by a man on horseback had a shorter haft and a smaller blade.

The **spear** came in a great variety of sizes, but as cavalry was not common in Scandinavia the use of the longer, heavier lance designed for mounted combat was uncommon. More widespread were the shorter infantry spears, of which there were two major forms. The first was the throwing javelin, which could vary in length from about 1m to 1.5m (3.28 to 4.9 feet). Then there was a heavier spear that was used as a thrusting and perhaps also as a hewing weapon; this was normally about 2m (6.5 feet) long. In the Icelandic *Njal's Saga* there is an interesting reference to a weapon called a 'spear axe'; no example of such a weapon has been found, but the description sounds like an early form of halberd. This is not unlikely, since the ancestor of the halberd is generally believed to have been a large two-handed axe.

The blades for ordinary thrusting spears could be short and narrow, resulting in a weapon which could be manoeuvred rapidly and needed a slimmer shaft, but several broader spearheads also survive. Some have flanges or 'wings' on their sides and are sometimes called 'boar spears'. The resulting weapons were heavier, and it would have been necessary to wield them using both hands. In such cases a man with a shield would have had to hang it by a broad strap or *guige*, taking the weight of the shield on his shoulders and freeing both hands to wield the spear.

LEFT **The remains of a mail shirt or hauberk from Romol, thought to date from the 12th century. The sleeves are missing but it seems unlikely that this armour was always sleeveless.**
RIGHT **Mail hauberk from Verdal, probably dating from the 12th or 13th century.**

Both the early medieval sagas and later medieval Scandinavian art show bows being used in various sorts of conflict. This was especially true in Norway, Sweden, the northern Atlantic settlements and Finland, which were less influenced by the emerging ideals of chivalry. Since the bow remained in common use for hunting it was widely available and many men knew how to use it. It is interesting to note that a form of bow later known as the 'Welsh longbow' has been found amongst Scandinavian grave goods from the Viking Age. Similar bows had existed since the Late Stone Age, and some historians have suggested that the longbow was introduced to the British Isles by Scandinavian raiders or merchants. The transition from the bow to the crossbow as a war weapon began in the 13th century, but would never amount to a complete replacement; the conventional 'self' bow remained in use in warfare at least to some extent.

### Southern Scandinavia 1100–1200

Denmark differed from the rest of Scandinavia in the rapidity and extent of the adoption of newer types of military equipment. Such items were largely imported, and Denmark already had close and well-established trading connections with the German Empire. This ensured that as the Middle Ages progressed economic links developed strongly, a process enhanced by the proximity of the main German cities of the Hanseatic League. As a result virtually the same arms and armour were used by the aristocracies of Denmark and Germany at approximately the same time.[1]

The styles of body armour worn in Denmark did not differ greatly from those used elsewhere in Scandinavia – the difference was one of availability. Consequently there was much wider use of the full mail hauberk and kite-shaped shield during the 11th and early 12th centuries. In Denmark we also find examples of various forms of helmet seen in Europe during the progression from the simple conical form to the fully enclosing 'great helm'; most of these are absent elsewhere in Scandinavia.

### The outlying territories

The medieval Scandinavian world included far-flung territories beyond Denmark, Sweden and Norway. They ranged from Greenland and Iceland to Finland which, though its people spoke a different language, was in several respects culturally part of the Scandinavian world. One

1 See MAA 310, *German Medieval Armies 1000–1300*

**Mail shirt from Estonia, 13th or 14th century. (Museum of Estonian History, Tallinn)**

could also include part of the eastern Baltic states, the large Baltic island of Gotland, and those areas in the far north of Norway, Sweden and Finland. The latter were populated by hunter-gatherer tribes known as *Samer* or *Skridfinnar,* who had been known to Mediterranean and other European writers since classical times. They also retained many pre-medieval methods of warfare, generally based on tribal organisation and a tribal way of thinking. Their equipment was not necessarily primitive but was simpler than that found in the rest of Scandinavia. For example northern hunters still used stone-tipped arrows and stone-bladed spears well into the early Middle Ages.

In the Baltic states and parts of Finland the main influences came from the east and south rather than Western Europe. The same influences were, to some extent, also felt in Sweden, where raids by Baltic peoples remained a reality into the 12th century. A period of raiding was followed by a period of important trading contacts across the Baltic, and these remained close throughout the rest of the Middle Ages. Such trading links are visible in the number of Eastern European items of weaponry found in Sweden, the presence of lamellar armour being the most dramatic. Meanwhile, there was no feudal cavalry élite amongst the indigenous peoples of the Baltic states or Finland – or at least, not one organised along the same lines as could be seen in the rest of Scandinavia. This situation changed with the establishment of Crusader states along the southern and eastern coasts of the Baltic during the 12th and 13th centuries, especially with the creation of the Teutonic Order and Order of the Sword Brethren, both of which were essentially German.

### The 13th century

The equipment of Western European fighting men underwent dramatic changes during the last decades of the 12th and the first half of the 13th century. This process was also felt in Scandinavia; and the typical time-lag in Scandinavia's acquisition of modern equipment shortened as the Middle Ages progressed. This was almost certainly a result of an extensive trade network that developed around the Baltic Sea and with the Hanseatic League.

The League was a trading union which brought together several large cities and enabled its members to obtain exclusive rights to trade in various goods. It also embraced a large part of the trade between Scandinavia, the Baltic and continental Europe. The growing economic strength of the Hanseatic cities eventually led them to become militarily as well as economically powerful, by hiring large numbers of mercenaries. Above all the Hanseatic League controlled by far the largest and most modern fleet, thus controlling transport by sea. Such naval, military and economic power meant that it was important for the belligerents in any northern war to maintain good relations with the Hanseatic League.

The most dramatic and fundamental change in the armour of this period was the introduction of **plate armour** at the close of the 13th century. This was not a wholly new idea in Scandinavia, where iron greaves had existed during the Migration Period, perhaps as a result of close links between some parts of Scandinavia and the steppe cultures of south-eastern Europe where comparable protections were more widespread. What was new was the addition of plate protections to other parts of the body, including the shoulders and knees of horsemen. Towards the end of the 13th century the coat-of-plates made its appearance. In Scandinavia the number of plates in such an armour could range from five to 40 or more; in the latter case the armour resembled the earlier lamellar armours seen in Scandinavia. The plates themselves were sewn or riveted onto a sleeveless coat, normally of waist length, made of leather or several layers of linen cloth. *Chausses* for the legs and mittens for the hands were similarly introduced to complete the armour of the 13th century Scandinavian mounted knight.

**Mail armour** now became readily available as substantial quantities were brought to the Scandinavian countries by trade, as the spoils of war, or having been passed from one generation to the next. Even in the 13th century the most common type still seems to have been the simple mail shirt, with sleeves that reached below the elbows and a skirt reaching to mid-thigh. The cut of such mail shirts remained broad so as not

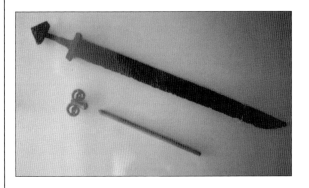

ABOVE **Sword from Iceland with one priority cutting edge, though the back also appears to be sharpened; 11th century. (National Museum, Reykjavik; on display at Keflavik Airport)**
RIGHT **Transitional form of sword from Skåne, with wide cutting blade and rounded point; 11th century. (Author's collection)**
FAR RIGHT **Early 12th century sword from Korsödsgården, Norway.**

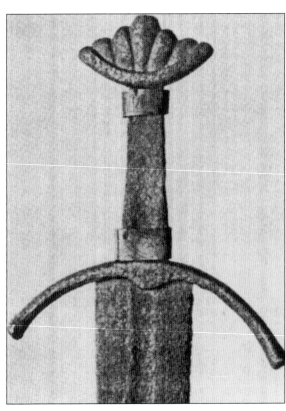

to hinder movement. Leather straps were used to tighten the mail around the arms, while a belt did the same around the waist.

The 13th century also saw the introduction of new styles of **helmet**. There is, however, no evidence that the transitional form of round or conical helmet with a face plate or rigid visor was ever used in Sweden or Norway. Instead it seems that there was a move directly from the conical to the fully enclosing 'great helm'. This sudden change can be seen on the seals used by Birger Jarl, which date from the mid-13th century. During this century the broad-brimmed 'kettle hat', 'war hat' or *chapel de fer* became the most widely used style among Scandinavian foot soldiers, and was subsequently adopted by some mounted knights as well. The brimmed chapel-de-fer did not obstruct breathing and the wearer retained a clear field of vision, while this simple form of helmet provided good protection. The types of chapel-de-fer seen in England and France had wide and sloping brims; in Scandinavia a different style evolved, which had almost flat brims that were not very wide. Perhaps this was a result of the fact that siege warfare was not common: when an infantryman expected to be fighting on foot in open battle or skirmishing, a relatively narrow brim served just as well, and was easier to manufacture.

The old round **shield** was gradually replaced – but never entirely so – by the smaller, so-called 'heater-shaped' shield. These could have straight or rounded upper edges, and had developed from the kite-shaped shield used by mounted knights in the 12th century. Shield bosses were similarly abandoned; the reinforced rim remained but was not always present, and a plain or unreinforced rim was now more common in illustrations. These shields appear to have been lighter and were designed to be used actively – i.e. to be wielded in parrying movements rather than hanging passively by a guige.

In Sweden the *Sörmlandslagen* stated that a warrior in a *hamna* or local levy district should bring with him a shield, a sword, a spear and an 'iron hat'; if he was able to, he should also bring mail or some other body armour, as well as bows and arrows. The **bow** and arrow, along with the **crossbow**, were now the most popular weapons in Scandinavia, and are often found in descriptions of battles. Meanwhile there were several reasons for a gradual change from the simple bow to the crossbow. First and foremost, for thousands of years the trading and export of animal pelts had been an important element in the Scandinavian economy. Hunting for such wild animals was easier when using a crossbow than a simple bow, and every man living in the Scandinavian countryside would have tried to obtain a crossbow for hunting. Furthermore, it was a lot quicker and easier to learn how to use a

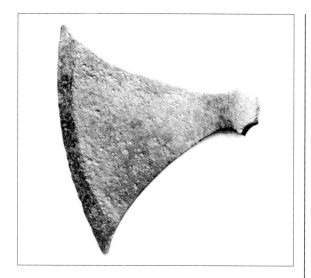
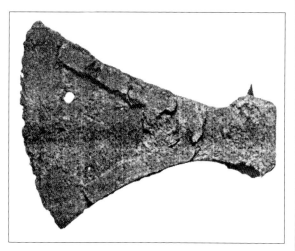

TOP **Scandinavian war-axe of typical 'Viking' form, from the 11th or 12th century. (British Museum, London)**
ABOVE **Scandinavian war-axe perhaps dating from the 12th century. (Private collection)**

crossbow – spanned by mechanical rather than muscle power – and the written sources state that a person could become a fairly competent cross-bowman in less than a week. This compared with the years required to become a truly proficient archer.

During siege warfare the crossbow proved to be a much more suitable weapon when shooting from behind fortifications, just as it was also easier to use than a self bow when shooting from behind natural cover in open battle. The most important factor behind the enthu-siastic adoption of the crossbow was probably a combination of this ease of use and great penetrating power: at close range a crossbow bolt or quarrel could puncture almost any form of armour.

More detailed infor-mation becomes available in the last decades of the 13th century. One of the most valuable doc-uments describes the arms and armour which members of the Norwegian king's Hird or 'royal following' were expected to have between 1273 and 1306. It may thus represent the level of equipment expected amongst members of most Scandinavian noble followings or from professional hired soldiers during this period. This document states that the royal *Hirdmen* should be protected by mail (presumably hauberks), plus *spaulders* to cover their shoulders, neck and perhaps upper arms. This was in addition to the required helmet and coif. They should possess a sword, spear, shield (presumably of the full-sized type) and a buckler or small hand-held shield. Mention was also made of the *platepanser*, which probably meant the coat-of-plates currently used in northern Germany – although some scholars believe that in late 13th century Norway the term referred to a variation on the padded *gambeson*. Finally, the Hirdmen were expected to have a bow – a requirement which clearly distinguishes the medieval Norwegian Hirdmen from military élites in most other parts of Western Europe, where the bow was regarded as a 'low class' weapon.

LEFT **Scandinavian spearhead from the 11th or 12th century. This slender-bladed weapon could perhaps have served as a javelin. (Private collection)**
TOP **Cast bronze mace head in the form of a grimacing face, Scandinavian, 13th century. (Private collection)**
ABOVE **Round shield from Rike, 13th century; diameter, 51cm (20ins). It is reinforced with a series of decorative iron straps riveted to the front.**

The *Lanslag* or 'code' of King Magnus Lagaböter of Norway (1263–1280), dating from 1274, indicates the different levels of equipment that men of various social or economic classes were supposed to have. The poorest man should possess a red shield with an iron rim around its sides, plus a spear and a sword or axe. Quite why the shield should be red is unclear, but might have had something to do with its leather covering. Men who were one step higher up the socio-economic ladder were supposed to bring the same equipment plus a helmet. Those in the next rank had the same, plus a mail shirt or a *panser*, probably meaning a coat-of-plates. Those men who were not free landowners should nevertheless bring a shield, a good spear, a broadaxe or at least a smaller axe.

A bronze aquamanile in the form of a fully armoured knight on horseback. It was probably imported into Denmark from northern Germany. (National Museum, Copenhagen)

### Tourneys and heraldry

There is evidence for the existence of tournaments in Scandinavia as early as the 13th century. For example, in the Norwegian tale of King Sverre, which dates from the first half of the 13th century, we learn that tourneys on horseback were well known. In 1275 there was a meeting between Magnus Birgersson and Erik Klipping where a tournament was again fought. These provided occasions for practising mounted combat and for strengthening social ties with other members of the aristocratic élite. Nor were there any modifications to suit Scandinavia's special circumstances; the tournament was imported into Scandinavia as a finished product, in which the local nobility attempted to copy the illustrious courts of France and England.

The use of heraldry as a means of recognising a member of the nobility, whether they be of the older landowning class or from the newer tax-exempted group of professional soldiers, existed by the mid-12th century. Its most obvious form was on seals attached to official documents. From the 13th century onwards heraldic designs are known from all the Scandinavian countries. These insignia used essentially the same heraldic forms and rules as were in force throughout the continent of Europe. On the other hand, it does seem that in 12th and early 13th century Scandinavia nobles or influential landowners adopted coats-of-arms of their own choosing rather than being granted the right to wear such arms by a superior authority.

# STRATEGY & TACTICS

The normal strategy used during medieval Scandinavian warfare was similar to that used during the Viking Age. Once again developments were slowed by the remoteness of Scandinavia, as well as by the fact that the Scandinavian kingdoms did not develop the landowning

Seal of Karl Döve Jarl, Sweden, early 13th century. The old-fashioned style of arms, armour and horse harness may result from the fact that this seal was based upon an earlier example made for Birger Brosa. (Riksarkivet, Stockholm)

aristocracy associated with mounted warfare, at least not until much later. As a consequence this development was so delayed that it only had practical military significance in Denmark. On the other hand, the adoption of what might be called the knightly ideal did have an impact on the self-image of the Scandinavian nobility, and this would prove significant in the cultural and social development of the Scandinavian nations.

In the 11th and 12th centuries the time and place of battle was very much a matter of agreement between both sides. A battlefield was selected and all participants rode or walked there; they would then array their forces and begin the fight. It was uncommon for a mounted warrior to actually fight on horseback before the late 12th or early 13th century. Even kings and their Hird or élite household troops would ride to the agreed location and then dismount to do battle. One notable exception – though of debatable reliability – is a description of the battle of Foteviken in 1154. Here, 60 knights supposedly routed a large levy of men on foot without other assistance. In reality it is more likely that one side had a contingent of cavalry who proved particularly effective in the subsequent battle.

In the 13th century the records indicate a genuine emergence of mounted knights of the kind seen in continental Europe. At the same time attributes, behaviour and attitudes associated with the broad European concept of 'chivalry' found their way into the Scandinavian aristocracy. Nevertheless, the significance of the mounted warrior should not be overstated, especially in Sweden and Norway. The numbers of landowning nobility who qualified for tax exemptions in return for service as mounted men remained small. Such mounted combat was an expensive affair, and considerable training was needed before a cavalryman could be effective. The total number of real fighting knights would always have remained small, though a larger number of squires or *svenner*, who were akin to the usual European men-at-arms, would probably have been available.

In early battles of the 11th and 12th centuries the largest or most ruthless body of men would usually win. Strategy was of less significance then the ancient concepts of valour and personal pride in battle. Losing well or honourably was still considered better than winning without the demonstration of valour which brought glory. In Denmark a hierarchical social order had already been established by the late 11th century, in contrast to the kings in Sweden and Norway, who had less personal power over their aristocracy. In the north during the 11th and 12th centuries the local nobility would often go to war followed by their own landholders, who rallied under a local warlord or chieftain. When the ruling king went to war he would have to try to gain the support of the greatest chieftains.

In a typical Scandinavian battle of this period the opposing armies formed two lines facing each other, or divided into two large groups

(continued on page 33)

THE BATTLE OF VÄNERN, 1063
1: Swedish nobleman
2: Swedish infantry archer
3: Norwegian nobleman

A

**B**

THE NORTH ATLANTIC COLONIES, LATE 11th CENTURY

1: Greenland settler
2: Icelandic high status warrior
3: Woman settler

DENMARK, 12th CENTURY
1: Danish knight, late 12th century
2: Danish infantryman, mid-12th century
3: Danish militia infantryman

C

SWEDEN & NORWAY, 12th CENTURY
1: Norwegian backwoodsman
2: Swedish crossbowman
3: Norwegian knight, late 12th century

D

THE KINGDOM OF THE ISLES, 12th CENTURY
1: Cavalryman
2: Armoured infantryman
3: Unarmoured infantryman

E

DENMARK, 13th CENTURY
1: Danish sergeant, mid-13th century
2: Danish rural levy
3: Danish knight, late 13th century

F

THE BATTLE OF HOVA, 1275
1: Swedish peasant levy infantryman
2: Swedish crossbowman, mid-13th century
3: Swedish royal retainer, late 13th century

G

NORWAY, LATE 13th CENTURY
1: Norwegian knight
2: Norwegian knight Björn Finnsons
3: Saami tribal warrior

on each side of a designated field of combat. In this type of confrontation the old 'shield wall' remained effective, as it allowed the use of the thrusting spear and the two-handed axe. Such formations were often several ranks deep, as would be seen in later medieval and early modern pole-arm infantry formations. Once the opposing shield walls closed with each other the outcome of the battle was decided in favour of whichever could endure the combat for the longest. Despite the element of premeditation over the time and place, it would be wrong to think of such bloody struggles as orderly affairs once the warriors came together.

At the start of the period under consideration there was really no true break with the strategy and tactics of the preceding Viking Age. Bows continued to be used in battle and remained very popular. The longbow was of course known, but was not the only type used; in fact, the normal war-bow was smaller than the fully developed longbow, having shorter range and less 'punch'.

During the late 12th and 13th centuries a new development appeared in Scandinavian battlefield tactics. This usually took the form of a large block of infantry, plus any available cavalry, which remained with the army's commanders at the rear of the main formation. From here it could support a threatened part of the line, prevent the line from being outflanked, or exploit weakness on one of the enemy's flanks.

Despite this development, the supposedly typical European 'knightly charge' was seldom used in Scandinavia. On those rare occasions when it was reported it often resulted in a very bloody affair for the cavalrymen involved. One of the main reasons for this lack of success may have been the fact that ordinary infantrymen from farms and households continued to train in the use of the 'shield wall' just as their ancestors

Scenes from the 'Massacre of the Innocents', on the so-called Golden Altar from Odder church near Århus, Denmark, 1225–1250. One shows a mail hauberk and chausses; the other, a fluted helmet and a fabric garment beneath the hem of a shorter hauberk.

had done. Generally speaking it remained true of Scandinavia, as of all other parts of the medieval world, that cavalry could not break a solid wall of infantrymen armed with pole-arms unless the foot soldiers' line faltered; as usual, the outcome usually hinged on the question of morale. This type of infantry training was, however, no longer common in the rest of Europe (except Italy), and generally had to be rediscovered in the 14th century. In Scandinavia the evidence of reported battles proves that resolute infantry were fully capable of stopping a mounted charge if properly equipped and disciplined.

In strategic terms a campaign was often intended to secure fertile farming land or to take control of strongpoints. It was not uncommon for an army to withdraw if the enemy gathered a sufficiently strong force to advance. Generally speaking, large battles were avoided or were risked

The seal of Birger Jarl from mid-13th century Sweden. The military equipment is by now within the same tradition as the rest of Western Europe. (Riksarkivet, Stockholm)

only when the odds looked particularly favourable. Seen from this perspective the warfare of this period might appear to resemble a game of chess, with a ruler manipulating the local aristocracy in an attempt to force them to join his faction. Another strategic aim was to remove potential members of the opposition from the game before the main enemy could attack. The sizes of the armies involved were small by continental European standards, usually being counted only in the hundreds with a well-equipped core of 50 or so mounted knights or *svenner* around the king. The rest of the army would be drawn from a general levy, hopefully with the addition of troops raised by sympathetic noblemen.

In what are now northern Sweden and Norway there were occasional clashes with the local hunter-gatherer tribes. These peoples were known for their extremely accurate marksmanship and their use of very strong bows. They also used skis to move further and faster than ordinary Swedish or Norwegian troops were able to do, and skis and sledges were in fact to become significant factors in medieval Scandinavian methods of warfare.

Scandinavia's lack of a fully developed feudal system was a left-over from the Viking era in which the primary social distinction was between the freeholders on one hand, and on the other the serfs or freemen who worked another man's land. Medieval Scandinavian society was also based upon a system of mutual recognition of power between noble families. The right to own land individually and freehold rather than holding it from the king in return for feudal obligations remained up to the reign of Gustav Vasa in the 16th century. It formed a major stumbling block during the later period of nation-building in both Sweden and Norway.

As already discussed, Denmark developed differently. After the reign of King Harold Bluetooth (c.958–c.987) the Danish nobility became accustomed to a growing feudal system which emphasised the ties of mutual obligation between the king and his subjects. A shared border and intense trade with Germany, as well as close trading links with Flanders, were the two major reasons for this development. In general Danish feudalism kept pace with developments seen in Germany, and consequently Denmark was a well-developed feudal kingdom by the middle of the 12th century. Here the mounted nobility formed the core of the king's army, while such a feature would not be seen in Sweden and Norway for up to one hundred and fifty years.

### Climate and topography

Another significant difference between warfare in Scandinavia and that in the rest of Western Europe concerned the 'fighting season'. In contrast with most of the rest of Europe, summer was not the only time for warfare. Since most of Scandinavia lacked any roads, and in many regions even tracks, movement was extremely slow. In the summer it could take four weeks for an army to move from Skåne to Stockholm, only 500km (310 miles) distant. By contrast, travel in winter using sledges and skis was easier, and the same journey could be made in two weeks or less; frozen lakes and rivers formed fast highways in the coldest months.

This climatic factor allowed small armies to undertake what could be called 'blitzkrieg' campaigns, but warfare was not only attempted in winter. During major wars it was normal to see another campaign carried out in summer, but summer campaigns often came to a swift end, especially when an army reached the point where one of the very few roads reached the deep forests that formed impenetrable walls between different parts of the country.

These natural constraints on land warfare naturally had an impact upon the development of naval warfare, and Denmark tried from an early date to develop a strong navy. A large part of Denmark's territory consisted of islands, and without control over the waterways between them it was impossible to hold the state together. On several occasions the Hanseatic League was employed by the Danish kings to ensure supremacy at sea. By contrast, Sweden and Norway had no such designs, and it was not until the 17th century that Sweden developed into anything like a maritime power.

## Field fortifications: the *bråte*

Throughout Scandinavia the lack of roads proved a blessing for the defender and a curse for the attacker. From a very early date a favourite defensive strategy was to send a small force quickly to cover the single road that led across a threatened frontier. There the troops would build a *bråte* across the road – an obstacle made of logs, brushwood and stones, which was often extended into the surrounding terrain to prevent the defensive position from being outflanked. Such an obstacle could stop cavalry in their tracks and could even prove a formidable hindrance for infantry. Normally the defenders remained behind the bråte, relying on bows, crossbows and pole-arms to keep the attackers at bay. If sufficient numbers were available to the defenders, attacks could be launched against the flanks of the invading forces using missile weapons with pole-arms for support.

An execution scene in an Icelandic manuscript said to date from the 13th century. (Stornun Arna Magnussonar a Islandi, Reykjavik)

The basic idea was very simple: to prevent a superior force from deploying to its full extent, and to deny it the benefit of its cavalry or superior numbers. Although such tactics could only be effective in heavily wooded or very rocky terrain where alternative routes did not exist, where these conditions did apply the use of the bråte proved so successful that a peasant levy could destroy professional mercenary or knightly units. On the other hand, speed was essential: vital crossing points had to be seized and the field works erected before the enemy arrived. Presumably it was because of the need for haste that mounted troops were often used to capture a bottleneck and then to hold it until the main body of infantry could come up.

# FIXED FORTIFICATIONS

Fortifications had been a prominent feature of Scandinavia during the Iron Age, but – unlike peoples who came into contact with the Roman Empire and Roman forms of architecture – Scandinavians did not construct significant stone fortifications prior to the 13th century. The first solid stone fortifications were, in fact, in the form of single standing towers that served as places of refuge for the inhabitants of a parish. Similar single standing towers would be the first solid stone fortifications to appear in western Russia a few decades later.

Earlier in the 11th century large earth and timber fortifications had been constructed, and there seem to be several similarities between these and the 'motte-and-bailey' form of early Norman fortifications in France and England. In Scandinavia the use of earth and timber defensive works remained very important until the end of the 15th century. This was to a large extent a result of Scandinavia's lack of roads and the fact that these countries were mostly covered with dense forests, divided by steep fjords and high mountains. Nature had already provided the best protection, while the remoteness of many centres of population from one another reduced the need for, and inhibited the development of, siege warfare. This lack of utility was the first reason that Scandinavia lagged well behind the rest of Europe in terms of fortification, rather than any ignorance on the part of Scandinavian commanders or military architects. The second significant factor was the relative weakness of Scandinavian monarchies (with the probable exception of Danish rulers) during the medieval period. For reasons already described, inadequate funds were available for major construction programmes; it was usually difficult for Scandinavian rulers to gather the tax revenues necessary for large castle projects funded from the royal purse.

Historical sources clearly indicate that many smaller cities and other communities did have their own modest fortifications. These generally consisted of ditches and earthworks, which were adequate under normal circumstances; they were not intended as a reliable defence against large and well-organised armies with military engineers capable of assaulting their gates. Rather, these simple fortifications marked the city limits, for the collection of taxes from those inside the walls and from merchants who wished to enter, as well as providing adequate protection against relatively weak local nobles or *stormän*. While these may have had designs upon the city, they generally lacked the military capability to fulfil such ambitions.

Swedish castles and fortifications remained on a small scale up until the very late Middle Ages. Some earlier Migration Period and Viking

'St Maurice', from a painted wooden panel of a reliquary in the Monastery at Lögum, Denmark, painted c.1300; it clearly shows the warrior-saint wearing a coat-of-plates.

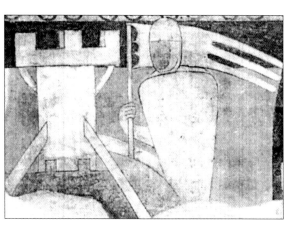

Age fortified settlements continued to be used, while new stone-built 11th and 12th century churches provided fortified assembly points for local populations. The same purpose was fulfilled by the so-called *Kastalerna*; these were stone towers, usually built in connection with churches as defensive structures. At an early date the churches and possibly also the Kastalerna had another important function, serving as storage places for taxes gathered by the nobility. The earliest towers were square and were constructed during the 12th century, though during the 13th a few round towers were built. Such Kastalerna were constructed in Sweden and Denmark, but none exist in Norway.

The earliest true stone castle in Sweden is at Näs, which was constructed in the 12th century. During the 13th century several castles were erected, coinciding with increasing efforts by the Swedish kings to gain effective control of the country. Other important castles were found at Kalmar, Borgholm, Nyköping, Stockholm, Gälakvist and Axvalla. The monarchy, now better organised with a legally codified relationship with the Swedish nobility, could rely on its sources of income to a greater extent than had previously been possible.

The functions of these castles varied. They served as centres of administration and tax gathering, as well as providing a focus for local trade. Furthermore, they demonstrated royal authority in the surrounding countryside. In addition to royal fortifications, others were built by bishops and there are several such ecclesiastical castles; an example still stands at Åhus in Skåne, southern Sweden. During this period there was a widespread effort to construct private fortifications, but these were on a very small scale compared to most Western European castles, and generally date from the 13th century.

The great medieval trading centre of Visby on the Baltic island of Gotland still has a magnificent wall around the old city. Begun in the 13th century as a protection against the surrounding countryside during an era of civil strife, it was completed in the early 14th century. Though this was not the only stone city wall in medieval Scandinavia, it is the only one which survives –

LEFT **Part of a wall-painting illustrating a motte and bailey castle, in which the tower has external supporting beams, as described in the writings of Saxo Grammaticus. It is in the church at Ål in Denmark, and dates from the first half of the 13th century.**

ABOVE **Hammerhus castle on the Danish island of Bornholm. This massive residential tower is probably the oldest part of the castle, its lower half dating from the mid-13th century. (A. Tuulse photograph)**

**A tower and an open-backed half-octagonal gate tower in the *Ringmur* of Visby on Gotland.**

Copenhagen and Stockholm both had impressive city walls, but only fragments remain.

In Denmark castle building started at an early date and we can still see many surviving fortified houses built by wealthy local farmers or members of the minor nobility. In the 10th century the so-called *Trelleborgarna* were erected. These were large, well-constructed earthworks topped with palisades. They were designed by the ambitious rulers of Denmark, most notably Harald Blåtand, to strengthen their control over the country, and remained in use well into the 11th century. The Trelleborgarna were then superseded by a series of small stone-built castles erected by the kings and the highest nobility.

The motte-and-bailey type of castle is represented by those at Sjørring Volde and Trindhöj, constructed in the 11th century; they were important enough to become royal castles, and were still listed as such in the 13th century *Jordebok* by the Danish King Valdemar Sejre. Although this type of construction was largely obsolete by the close of the 12th century in the rest of Western Europe, it remained in use in Scandinavia for a very long time – as late as the 14th century in northern Sweden. Another special kind of Scandinavian fortification was a motte tower resting on stilts and supported by sloping beams at the sides. A rare form of fortification were the small wooden coastal towers erected as look-out points to observe the sealanes.

King Valdemar the Great of Denmark also erected Sprogö tower, a simple square structure within a square wall without towers. Another interesting Scandinavian castle is at Törnborg, which originally formed part of a chain of fortifications protecting Stora Bält until 1425. This fortification originally consisted of a square tower inside a wall lacking towers. The most impressive 12th century castle in Denmark is at Vordingborg. Built by Valdemar the Great, it consisted of an irregular four-sided wall and a square gate tower plus corner towers; these parts of the existing castle date from around 1250. In Denmark several examples of the *palatium* were built by the nobility, the Church and the king; these were primarily intended as dwellings rather than as defensive locations, though fortifications were often added to some degree.

Norway was, like Sweden, behind Denmark when it came to the construction of large fortifications of the continental European type. Here there were examples of houses designed to provide some measure of defence as well as a suitable place to live. In Norway there was also an intensive church-building programme, and again it is likely that in some cases the churches provided a measure of local protection. In Trondheim, for example, the archbishop built a hall which measured 21m x 11m (68.8 x 36 feet), with a small, easily defensible entrance and small windows. During the 13th century an extra wall was built around this hall and its adjacent buildings to create a small urban fortress.

One of the gates in the *Ringmur* or curtain wall of the town of Visby, on the Swedish island of Gotland. Most of this wall was started in the late 13th century, though it may have incorporated earlier work.

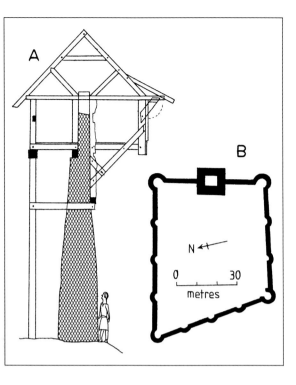

In 1182 King Sverre built the castle of Sion, which is today called Sverresborg. It consisted of a small gate tower, a dry moat and a ring or curtain wall. In Oslo construction work on the famous Akershus was begun in 1290 by King Håkon while he was still duke of that city. This is a much more advanced design then the older ring-wall castles and resembles the continental European model, though on a smaller scale. One of its most interesting characteristics is the fact that a large part of the castle is constructed of bricks and mortar, which is early for such a large Scandinavian fortification.

Kings Håkon IV, Håkon V and Magnus Lagaböter all built extensively at Tönsberg. Here the castle's outer ring-wall measures 340m x 170m (1,110 x 557 feet), while the inner walls measure 125m x 70m (410 x 230 feet). In addition there was a large gate tower, and a second tower which measured approximately 16m x 13m (52.5 x 42.6 feet). Clearly there was extensive building in many parts of Norway, perhaps because Trondheim was a major place for Christian pilgrimage in northern Europe; in fact, between 1150 and 1450 the bishop of Trondheim was the most significant Norwegian castle builder next to the king.

**(A) Section through the eastern part of the curtain wall of Vordingsborg castle in Denmark, showing a reconstruction of the timber walkway and hoarding on top of the wall. The remains of the 13th century wooden walkway and its roof were found in the castle moat during an archaeological excavation. It had been covered in hide as a defence against fire, and included a movable hatch through which archers could shoot. (After Smid)**

**(B) The plan of Nyborg castle in Denmark. Constructed in the 1170s, it was later enlarged by Valdemar Sejr. The construction consisted of an irregular four-sided enclosure with flanking towers, though the oldest structure was the rectangular tower incorporated into the east wall. A *palatium* or palatial dwelling was added before 1250.**

## Siege warfare

Siege warfare in Scandinavia between the 11th and the end of the 13th century was rarely conducted in the manner seen elsewhere in Europe. The most common procedure was that once a siege had begun, the garrison commander would be offered a chance to surrender. This he would normally refuse; after two weeks or so new negotiations would be arranged, and the garrison commander would usually offer to surrender if his liege lord had not sent relief within a fortnight or a month. Nevertheless, such sieges were very uncommon in Scandinavia. The main reasons were that there were so few places to besiege, and few military leaders other than the king had the forces to conduct sieges. Since the king depended upon the good will of the nobility in all military matters, at least until the second half of the 13th century, he was unlikely to alienate them by attacking their fortifications.

The weapons used during the few sieges that did take place included missile weapons; but it was equally common for besiegers to establish a picket line and construct hasty field defences out of range of the walls, where they would sit down and wait for the fortified place to surrender. Scandinavian siege warfare suffered from a general shortage of skilled engineers to construct siege machinery. This would, however, change in the 14th century and there are, in fact, no clear records of the use of siege engines in Scandinavia before that period. A *blida* was then recorded, this being a large stone-throwing device which could hurl missiles of up to 50kg or even 100kg (110 & 220 pounds). The battering ram was not apparently used until the 15th century, perhaps because of a lack of things to batter.

# FURTHER READING

Alm, J., 'Europeiska armborst: En översikt', *Vaaben-historisk Aarboger,* V/b (1947), 107–255

Andersson, Ingvar, *A History of Sweden* (London, 1955)

Bergpórsson, Páll, *The Wineland Millenium; Saga and Evidence* (Reykjavik, 2000)

Christensen, A.E., 'Denmark between the Viking Age and the time of the Valdemars', *Medieval Scandinavia,* I (1966), 33–48

Christiansen, E., *The Northern Crusades: The Baltic and the Catholic Frontier 1100–1525* (London, 1980)

Ekroll, Öystein, *Med kleber og kalk* (Oslo, 1997)

Gjerset, Knut, *History of Iceland* (London, 1922)

Gjerset, Knut, *History of the Norwegian People* (New York, 1915)

Helle, Knut, *Norge blir en stat 1130–1319* (Bergen & Oslo, 1974)

Holand, Hjalmar R., *Norse Discoveries & Explorations in America 982–1362* (New, York 1940) – this work includes controversial evidence which some people believe indicates a greater degree of Scandinavian contact with North America than is generally accepted.

Jutikkala, Eino, *A History of Finland* (London, 1962)

Kaufmann, J.E., & H.W. Kaufmann, *The Medieval Fortress: Castles, Forts and Walled Cities of the Middle Ages* (London, 2001)

Liebgott, Niels-Knud, *Dansk Middelalder arkeologi* (Copenhagen, 1989)

Musset, Lucien, *Les Peuples Scandinaves au Moyen Age* (Paris, 1951)

Musset, L., 'Problèmes militaires du Monde Scandinave (VII–XIIe siècle)', in *Settimane di Studi del Centro Italiano di Studi sull'Alto Medioevo* (Spoleto, 1968), 229–291

Nicolle, David, *Medieval Warfare Sourcebook,* (London, 1999)

Oakshotte, Ewart, *The Sword in the Age of Chivalry* (Woodbridge, 1998)

Oakshotte, E., *The Archaeology of Weapons* (Woodbridge, 1999)

Oakshotte, E., *Records of the Medieval Sword* (Woodbridge, 1998)

Rausing, G., *The Bow: Some Notes on its Origins and Development* (London, 1967)

Sawyer, Peter & Birgit, *Medieval Scandinavia* (Minneapolis, 1993)

Tuulse, Armin, *Castles of the Western World* (London, 1958)

Urban, William, *The Baltic Crusade* (Chicago, 1994)

Yates, Anna, *The Viking Discovery of America* (Reykjavik, 1993)

A reconstruction of the castle of Akkershus in Norway. This castle was started in the closing years of the 13th century by Håkon V before he was crowned king. (After E.S. Larsen)

# THE PLATES

## A: THE BATTLE OF VÄNERN, 1063

At the battle of Vänern between Sweden and Norway in 1063, both sides entered combat on foot and fought in a traditional 'Viking' manner. The battle ended when – according to *King Harald's Saga* – the Norwegians charged downhill against the 'lightly clad' Gotlanders.

### A1: Swedish nobleman

By the mid-11th century much of Scandinavia was already under strong technological and military influence from continental Europe. As a result styles of arms and armour associated with Germany, England and France were coming into widespread use. This Swedish nobleman or élite warrior has a so-called 'Norman' type of helmet, though the slight upwards curl at the base of the nasal might indicate that it was imported from Germany or elsewhere in central Europe. The leather laces emerging from beneath the back of this helmet are to tighten the lining around his head. His tunic is of a style seen throughout most of Western and Northern Europe, though the richly embroidered material around its edges has been imported from the Islamic world, probably via Russia or Eastern Europe. His loose-fitting trousers are, however, in an older and traditionally Scandinavian style; their striped material has again been imported from the East. The simple mail hauberk is made of large iron rings and is of typical though old-fashioned Western European style; the slits at the sides of the hem indicate that it was primarily designed for infantry combat. The sword scabbard protrudes from a hole in the left hip of the hauberk and is probably supported by a baldric rather than a waist belt. The plain undecorated sword is a slashing rather than thrusting weapon, and has a hilt which is in the general European rather than the earlier Scandinavian 'Viking' tradition. The large round shield is more old-fashioned; its hypothetical decoration is based upon that seen on the hilt of a similarly dated Scandinavian sword from Finland.

### A2: Swedish infantry archer

Several aspects of this man's clothing indicate the survival of earlier Scandinavian fashions which differed from those of most of continental Europe. These include his woollen hat, and the loose-fitting three-quarter-length trousers which are worn over more conventional longer trousers. His archery equipment is comparable to that seen in many other parts of Europe, with the notable exception of the bow itself. This is an all-wood 'flat bow' of a type believed to have been characteristic of various northernmost parts of Europe; in this powerful weapon the curvature is concentrated in two areas

Rear views of two of the foot soldiers from the Lewis chess pieces, made in the Kingdom of the Isles during the 12th century; see Plate E. Both helmets have pendant cheek and neck protections, in one case perhaps made of hardened leather. (British Museum, London)

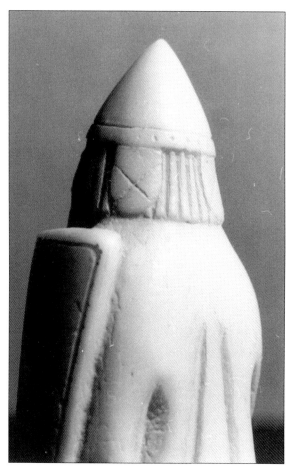

**One of the Lewis chess pieces showing a foot soldier wearing a full mail hauberk and a fluted helmet which lacks cheek and neck pieces, presumably because the mail coif offers adequate protection. (British Museum, London)**

while the bow itself looks very broad when seen from the front. The man's round wooden shield, which only has a leather covering on the front, is hung low on his hip by its leather guige so as to be out of the way while shooting. The archer's close combat weapon is a simple spear whose iron blade has some degree of silver inlay around its very long socket.

### A3: Norwegian nobleman

Norway was second to Denmark in accepting military and technological influences from outside Scandinavia, and this nobleman's arms, armour and clothing are still of old styles. His conical iron helmet is made of four segments riveted inside an iron frame; it would also have a nasal at the front. His simple short-sleeved mail hauberk includes an integral mail coif, while the short hem is slit front and back, perhaps indicating that it was made in Germany and originally

intended for combat on horseback. His loose-fitting, brightly coloured woollen trousers are traditionally Scandinavian, though tightened around his leg by cross-gartering. The leather belt has numerous silvered bronze stiffening plates, while the scabbard is attached by two short leather straps – both features that might indicate contact with Eastern Europe, Russia or even the nomadic Turkish cultures of the steppes. The broad sword clearly has one priority cutting edge, which curves towards its tip, though the back of the blade also appears to be sharpened. These contradictory features could betray a residual influence from the East, where Scandinavian soldiers as well as merchants were still in close contact with Russia, the Byzantine Empire and the Islamic world. The substantial iron hilt of this weapon, with its simple inlaid silver decoration, is, however, fully within an early medieval European or 'Viking' tradition. The oval or 'rounded rectangular' shape of the flat wooden shield may again indicate Eastern or Byzantine influence; note that it is still held in the fist, with an iron boss to protect the hand, rather than by a pair of riveted leather straps.

## B: THE NORTH ATLANTIC COLONIES, LATE 11th CENTURY

Whether the Scandinavian settlers, explorers and hunters living in Greenland still made regular visits to the North American mainland in the 12th and 13th centuries is unclear. It would, however, seem likely that they cut timber in what is now Labrador, and hunted seals, whales and other marine mammals around the north-eastern islands of Canada. The Greenland colonies themselves survived for many centuries, and Iceland was, of course, never abandoned.

### B1: Greenland settler

No Scandinavian military equipment seems yet to have been found in Greenland or North America. It thus remains unclear whether the Norse settlers continued to use very old-fashioned equipment such as this man's Viking period iron helmet, or were wealthy enough to import more modern arms and armour from Europe. The low-domed helmet seen here is strengthened with a crosspiece over the top and has an open face mask riveted to the front. Similarly the wearing of a substantial polar bear skin cloak is presumed rather than proven. The man has also been given traditional Scandinavian forms of clothing rather than the continental European fashions now coming into use in Scandinavia. His weapons consist of a long-bladed dagger or late form of *seax*, a substantial spear and three lighter javelins.

### B2: Icelandic high status warrior

Wood carvings from Iceland indicate that a distinctive form of 12th century helmet was used here, as it was in Norway and the Norse-dominated western islands of what is now Scotland. These came in a variety of conical forms and were distinguished by pendant ear flaps plus a similar pendant neck protection. The Icelandic carvings also show a long nasal bar, which was not always present back in Scandinavia. The helmet shown here may either be of two halves joined by a ridge piece from front to back, or this ridge may merely be a reinforcement over a one-piece helmet bowl. This high status Icelandic warrior wears a very simple form of short-sleeved mail hauberk which lacks a head-protecting coif. His sword scabbard and seax or dagger sheath both hang from his waist belt by leather thongs, which is unlike the systems seen elsewhere in Western Europe.

### B3: Woman settler

Female costume in the Scandinavian colonies of Iceland and Greenland seems to have remained traditionally Scandinavian during the 11th century, but gradually became the same as that of Western Europe in the 13th and 14th centuries. The apron-like garment worn over both the front and back of this woman's dress was characteristic of these northern lands, whereas the distaff and spindle she uses to spin thread were almost universal.

## C: DENMARK, 12th CENTURY

During the 12th century the arms, armour and costume of Denmark, as the most 'Europeanised' of the Scandinavian kingdoms, became virtually indistinguishable from those of northern Germany. The country remained, however, old-fashioned in comparison with its southern neighbour.

### C1: Danish knight, late 12th century

The segmented iron helmet has a very early form of fixed face guard or visor; this was a precursor of the normally flat-topped 'great helm' already seen in the German Empire,

Seal of Håkon Håkonsson, 13th century. The rider wears an early form of flat-topped 'great helm' with a face guard, but only limited neck protection.

France, England and Italy. Beneath the helmet he wears a mail coif forming an integral part of his hauberk, plus a chin- and throat-covering mail ventail laced to leather thongs on his left temple. The hauberk also incorporates mail mittens with soft leather palms, the latter slit so that the man can take the mittens off his hands; note the tightening laces around the wrists. The surcoat with very broad three-quarter-length sleeves is in a German fashion. It may incorporate substantial padding over the shoulders and chest, accounting for the very raised shoulderline, though this may also be caused by a thickly padded gambeson worn beneath the hauberk – this is visible below the hem of the mail. The legs are protected by mail chausses of the form which are laced around the front of his legs and over his feet, rather than covering the entire limb. His sword is so typically German that it was probably imported from that country; his equally typical late 12th century European kite-shaped shield is reinforced with slender iron cross-pieces held in place by a small iron boss.

### C2: Danish infantryman, mid-12th century

The only two features which might identify this infantryman as Scandinavian are the blade of his short thrusting spear, which has reverse-curved 'wings' and is based upon an example found in Finland, and his helmet. The latter has the forward-tilted crown widely seen across much of Europe, but the strengthening bar or frame up the front and the pointed finial are based upon a 12th century Scandinavian wood carving. The rest of his clothing and military equipment are typically European of the mid- to late 12th century, including a simple mail hauberk; a broad

Detail from mid-13th century painted wooden panel showing 'The Story of St Mary of Antioch', in the timber stave church at Ål in Norway. Note the brimmed *chapel-de-fer* helmets worn over coifs, and the 'kite' shields with straight upper edges. (Jo. Sellaeg photograph)

slashing sword with a tapering blade, in a scabbard attached to the divided ends of a knotted sword-belt; and a very large leather-covered wooden kite-shaped shield. The simple heraldic motif on the surface of this shield is another and highly visible example of how the military personnel of Denmark had been drawn into Western European feudal traditions.

### C3: Danish militia infantryman

The similarity between this militiaman's arms and armour and that illustrated on the earlier Bayeux Tapestry is not a coincidence. The Anglo-Saxons and Anglo-Danes in Harold of England's army were almost entirely within a Nordic military tradition, whereas their Norman opponents were equipped in a more advanced French style. This man's one-piece conical helmet with its integral nasal bar is of a type popularly known as a 'Norman helmet' but which was common throughout almost the whole of Europe. His mail hauberk has the side-slit hems normally associated with infantry combat. The large round shield and large-bladed war-axe are, however, typically Danish.

### D: SWEDEN & NORWAY, 12th CENTURY

During the 12th century Norway and Sweden were even more old-fashioned in terms of arms and armour than was Denmark. These supposedly archaic traditions reflected their distinctive military and economic circumstances. Norway, for example, was certainly not an inwards-looking or backward kingdom; its overseas territories were still expanding and the wealth produced by the products of the Arctic world was considerable. It might, in fact, be true to say that Norway's preference for seemingly old-fashioned arms and armour was a conscious choice of military equipment which served the purposes at hand rather than merely imitating that of more powerful states in continental Europe. Some of the distinctive features seen in Swedish military equipment similarly reflected that country's continuing close links with lands along the eastern shore of the Baltic Sea and, indeed, with Russia.

### D1: Norwegian backwoodsman

The distinctive Scandinavian habit of fitting additional protective elements to the rim of a helmet would continue throughout the Middle Ages. Sometimes these included neck and cheek pieces as well as the usual nasal bar, sometimes only one or two of these elements were present. This frontiersman has no armour other than his helmet, which is of a tall conical form with a rigid neck bar at the back in addition to a nasal bar. These are shown on at least one Norwegian wood carving and appear to be extensions of a reinforcing band which runs across the helmet from front to back. The band itself may, however, form a frame with the horizontal brow band, to which the two halves of a two-piece helmet bowl may have been riveted. The man's heavy cloak, perhaps of wolfskin, would provide additional protection. He has a large kite-shaped shield of leather-covered wood with a small iron boss, a simple thrusting spear, and a sword with a somewhat unusual form of hilt – its bronze pommel is in an archaic style, while the sharply curved bronze quillons look remarkably up-to-date. Since he carries the scabbarded sword in his hand, its attached swordbelt is wrapped and tied around it.

### D2: Swedish crossbowman

The mixed equipment used by this man illustrates the competing Western and Eastern influences which would be seen in Sweden for many years to come. His helmet, with its forward-angled crown, seems very Western, though the style itself is probably of Middle Eastern Islamic or Byzantine origin. His lamellar cuirass is very clearly of Eastern inspiration and may in fact be an import from Russia, Prussia or Lithuania. His kite-shaped shield with its rounded top edge is Western though old-fashioned; paradoxically, the shape probably originated in the Middle East as an infantry protection, rather than as a cavalryman's shield as it was normally used in Western Europe. Even this man's apparently typically Western European crossbow had been reintroduced into Europe as a war weapon from the Islamic Middle East during the 11th century, though it certainly reached Scandinavia via Western Europe rather than directly from the East.

### D3: Norwegian knight, late 12th century

By the late 12th century the fully armoured knightly cavalry élite of Norway were almost entirely within the mainstream of Western European military tradition, but surviving pictorial sources such as church tapestries and wood carvings suggest that the country was still old-fashioned. The equipment used by this horseman would have appeared at least 50 years out of date in France. The most obviously archaic feature is his mail hauberk, which lacks either a mail ventail to protect his throat or mittens for his hands. The helmet is a hypothetical reconstruction based upon surviving pictorial sources; the four segments are riveted directly to one another in a manner more typical of Eastern Europe, and topped by a small riveted finial. The very large form of kite shield was still used elsewhere in Western Europe but was already being relegated to second line cavalry. The Norwegian knight's horse harness betrays lingering Baltic or Eastern European influence rather than being merely old-fashioned; the saddle, for example, lacks the raised cantle and pommel of the typical knightly saddle. Its continued use in this part of Scandinavia must surely reflect the different forms of combat seen here, with infantry still dominating, while fighting on horseback may usually have been a matter of skirmishing and raiding rather than the massed knightly charges seen further south.

## E: THE KINGDOM OF THE ISLES, 12th CENTURY

The Norse-ruled Kingdom of the Isles and Kingdom of Man in what are now western Scotland and the Irish Sea seem in some respects to have been more cut off from the main-stream of medieval European military developments than were the more distant Scandinavian colonies in Iceland and Greenland. This was probably because the Celtic and Norse regions of northern and western Britain and Ireland formed a self-contained cultural world, whereas Iceland and Greenland were direct off-shoots of Scandinavian culture. The figures illustrated here are all based upon the Lewis chessmen, a remarkable collection of over ninety 12th century walrus ivory chess pieces found on the Outer Hebridean island of Lewis.

### E1: Cavalryman

Since a few of the Lewis chessmen are clearly shown wearing mail armour indicated by cross-hatching, those figures whose outer garments are smooth can be assumed to lack such armour, unless is was worn beneath a fabric outer garment. This horseman lacks any body armour except for a helmet, with the pendant cheek and neck protections so typical of 12th and even 13th century Scandinavian warriors. Most of the Lewis helmets lack nasals, but the one upon which this horseman is based could be interpreted as incorporating one. A very large shield was obviously necessary when no body armour was worn, though the flat-topped kite form seen here is actually quite modern under the circumstances. The sword with its all-bronze hilt is old-fashioned, however; it is based upon an example found on the other side of the Norse-Scandinavian world, close to the Baltic Sea. The size of the horses or ponies portrayed in the Lewis chess set should not be interpreted too literally; nevertheless, it would seem that the animals available in 12th century western Scotland and the Isles were even smaller than those used in Scandinavia itself. The clear representation of a very high, almost rectangular saddle pommel and cantle might indicate influence from England, itself under very strong French military influence. The exceptionally long saddle blanket may, on the other hand, be a survival of an older local tradition of horse harness, since it looks virtually the same as that seen in early medieval Pictish art from Scotland.

### E2: Armoured infantryman

Amongst the foot soldiers in the Lewis find are a few who are clearly meant to be wearing mail hauberks, and some of these also lack helmets. Since the mail hauberks are shown reaching to the ground (perhaps because the carving of even short legs would have made the chess pieces unstable), the result is a stumpy, almost dwarf-like figure covered in mail from head to toe. In reality it seems unlikely that even the longest mail hauberk would have reached below the mid-shins, as reconstructed here. The shape of the shield is very old-fashioned; and the warrior has been given a substantial war-axe. The Lewis figures are armed with swords and spears but written and archaeological records indicate that the 'Viking' axe remained a popular weapon in this part of the British Isles.

### E3: Unarmoured infantryman

Most of the foot soldiers among the Lewis chessmen lack body armour, as do the horsemen, and one of these has been reconstructed here. His shield, sword and sword-belt could have come straight from 12th century Scandinavia, or from several other parts of Western Europe. His helmet is an attempt to interpret what appears to be one of the earliest representations of a brimmed war-hat or *chapel-de-fer* seen in European art. Such helmets were known in the Byzantine Empire at an earlier date, and may have reached Scandinavia from that direction. If the brimmed helmet was known to Scandinavian warriors as early as the Viking Age, it may have been the reality behind those otherwise unexplained and surely misinterpreted 'winged helmets' for which the Vikings are popularly renowned. The brimmed helmet provides additional protection, especially when fighting on foot – and the wish for such protection had long been seen in the added cheek- and neck-pieces that often feature in medieval Scandinavian art.

## F: DENMARK, 13th CENTURY

During the 13th century Denmark played a major role in the Baltic Crusades. These were directed against the pagan peoples of what are now the Baltic states of Lithuania, Latvia, Estonia and Finland, plus the Prussians of northern Poland and Russia's Baltic enclave of Kaliningrad. During this period Danish arms, armour and horse harness largely mirrored those of neighbouring Germany, though there was also a continuing preference for the brimmed war-hat form of helmet.

### F1: Danish sergeant, mid-13th century

This relatively lightly armoured cavalry sergeant wears a one-piece iron war-hat or *chapel-de-fer* of a kind that would remain popular throughout Scandinavia for many years. It is worn over a separate mail coif, which appears to have a thickly padded or quilted fabric shoulder and neck protection sewn or laced to its interior. The three-quarter-length sleeved surcoat is worn over a mail hauberk with slightly longer but not full length sleeves. A quilted *gambeson* or *aketon* is just visible beneath the mail hauberk. There is no protection for the hands, lower legs or feet. His broad but short shield of the so-called 'heater' shape bears a simple heraldic motif, and is held by two internal straps plus a leather *guige* strap around his neck and shoulders. In

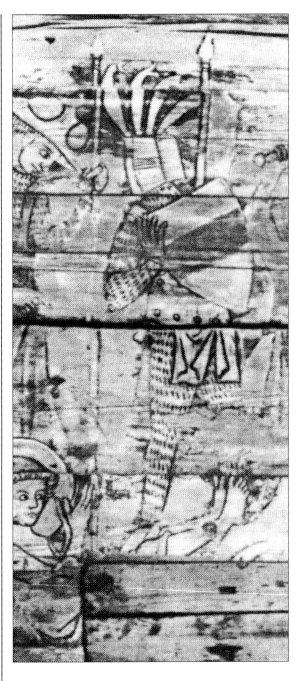

**Detail from a wall-painting in the old wooden church at Södra Råda in Sweden, dating from the late 13th or early 14th century. The figure with the flat-topped 'great helm' and simple heraldic shield wears a coat-of-plates over his hauberk; cf Plate G3.**

Northern and Western Europe. His only protections are a close-fitting iron helmet of *cervelliere* form, and a rather small round wooden shield, here slung on his back. He is armed with a longbow, which was normally regarded as a hunting rather than a war weapon during the 13th century, plus a large war-axe.

### F3: Danish knight, late 13th century
In complete contrast to the simple peasant levy, this knight of the last years of the century has the latest arms and armour imported from Germany. These include a transitional form of 'great helm' – not yet the round-topped type but already made from relatively few substantial riveted plates. Over a short mail hauberk with long sleeves and integral mail mittens, here thrown back to his wrists, he wears an early form of coat-of-plates. This consists of a series of iron plates riveted to an outer fabric cover and probably also to an inner lining of fabric or soft leather. In the early German and Scandinavian style the fabric cover is extended to form a sort of apron at the front and back, thus serving the purpose of a surcoat. The interior grip straps and guige of his shield can also be seen. In addition to a long cavalry lance, he is armed with a heavy bronze mace whose head is in the form of a grimacing face; this is carried in a loop on his left hip. His sword and scabbard are meanwhile slung from the cantle of his saddle. The fabric caparison over his horse appears to be decorative and heraldic rather than protective, though there is some form of semi-rigid or thickly padded protection over the front of the horse's head beneath the cloth.

### G: THE BATTLE OF HOVA, 1275
On 14 June 1275 a battle was fought between the Swedish King Valdemar Birgersson and his brother Magnus, who had the support of Denmark. The army of the victorious pretender Magnus numbered between 1,000 and 1,200; the size of King Valdemar Birgersson's defeated army is unknown. As a result of this campaign Valdemar was deposed and Magnus took the Swedish throne.

### G1: Swedish peasant levy infantryman
Little is known about the equipment used by the rural levies of Sweden or Norway, except that it seems to have been rudimentary and old fashioned. The man shown here wears a fur-lined hat of a kind which appears, though not very clearly, on some 13th century Scandinavian panel paintings; it is similar to some hats seen in medieval Russia and must have reflected the harsh winter climate of both regions. The fur cape may have provided a limited degree of protection. He also has a large but very old-fashioned form of kite shield on his back. His weapons consist of a spear with so-called 'anti-penetration wings' or lugs below the blade, and a relatively light axe thrust into his belt – probably a work-tool rather than a purpose-made weapon.

### G2: Swedish crossbowman, mid-13th century
The quality of this crossbowman's arms and armour indicate that he is a professional soldier rather than a member of some militia levy. His tall fluted helmet is of one-piece construction, with a riveted browband which extends into a broad nasal. The mail coif which covers his head and shoulders has been pulled up over this nasal, which would make breathing easier as well as protecting his mouth. In addition to a simple mail hauberk with three-quarter-length sleeves he has mail *chausses*, worn inside his leather boots.

addition to a spear bearing the Danish banner – which, according to tradition, fell to earth during a Danish Crusade – he is armed with a large cavalry sword and a small dagger.

### F2: Danish rural levy
Evidence suggests that the rural levy in Denmark was generally poorly equipped, as was the case in most parts of

The large shield would not be regarded as particularly old-fashioned for an infantry crossbowman, who needed such protection during the slow process of reloading his weapon. His relatively short infantry sword is modern, as is the crossbow, which now incorporates a powerful stave of composite construction.

### G3: Swedish royal retainer, late 13th century

This Swedish knight has an unusual mixture of new style and old-fashioned military equipment. His flat-topped 'great helm' is of a type that would be considered mid- or even early 13th century elsewhere in continental Europe; it is worn over a simple mail coif. Beneath this is a very modern coat-of-plates; this is made in the same way as that worn by F3, but here the extended fabric covering forms shorter aprons at front and back. The man's mail hauberk also lacks mittens, though may be intended to be worn with the separate mail gloves which were just coming into fashion. His mail chausses cover the entire leg, front and back, and have leather soles beneath the feet. His shield is again in the latest style, as is his sword and scabbard; the hilt is of a highly decorated form.

## H: NORWAY, LATE 13th CENTURY

During the medieval period the Kingdom of Norway gradually extended its authority northwards into territory inhabited by the nomadic *Saami* or Lapps. This did not usually involve major military operations, though there were local clashes between the two peoples.

### H1: Norwegian knight

Various forms of brimmed helmet are shown in 13th century Norwegian art. A few appear to include protective earflaps similar to those seen on some morion-type helmets in the 16th century; equally, they might be meant to indicate that a fabric coif was being worn under the helmet. Beneath the helmet this knight has a mail coif which fits inside what has been interpreted as the thickly padded raised collar of a mail hauberk. The latter includes mail mittens; and the man's arms are also protected by early forms of metallic or hardened leather *couters* over the elbows. In addition to mail chausses over his legs he has quilted fabric *cuisses* made in the same manner as the padded gambeson beneath his hauberk. The seemingly old-fashioned kite shield may have been needed because the rider still lacks semi-rigid body armour such as a coat-of-plates. The thickly quilted horse caparison offers the animal some degree of protection.

### H2: Norwegian knight Björn Finnsons

This figure is based upon his damaged effigy slab in Trondheim Cathedral. He wears a typically Norwegian 13th century brimmed helmet worn over a quilted coif or arming cap. No other form of armour is visible; his simple, unpadded sleeveless surcoat is, however, closed at the front with a large decorative pin brooch. Whereas his soft leather sword-belt is undecorated, the knightly belt drawn tightly around his waist has numerous decorative bronze stiffeners, and a very long end hanging down the front. The spear, sword and scabbard are again simple and undecorated, while his leather-covered wooden shield has four large rivet heads securing the internal grip straps and guige.

### H3: Saami tribal warrior

Little is known about the costume and military equipment of the largely peaceful Saami people who inhabited the

**Incised effigial slab of the Norwegian knight Björn Finnsons, late 13th century; cf Plate H2. (in situ, Cathedral, Trondheim)**

northernmost parts of Scandinavia. It is likely to have been very similar to that of the Finns and other northern Baltic peoples further east. For this reason the Saami hunter has been reconstructed as clad in a simple thick woollen tunic and loose-fitting woollen trousers, a thick sleeveless coat of wolfskin, and a cape of reindeer hide. Around his neck he wears an animal-shaped bronze decoration taken from a Russian horse harness; this was found by archaeologists in a medieval Saami dwelling place and may have been used as a totem or good luck charm. The man is armed with three simple hunting javelins and a bronze-headed mace thrust into his belt. This simple weapon was clearly popular among the neighbouring Finns and so it seems likely that the nomadic Saami acquired some. His skis are based upon medieval examples found in Russia. They would have been used with a single ski-pole; this was the method of cross-country skiing until modern times.

# INDEX